Living Habitats

Written by Jon Richards • Illustrated by Josy Bloggs

W
FRANKLIN WATTS
LONDON · SYDNEY

This edition published in Great Britain
in 2022 by Hodder & Stoughton
Copyright © Hodder & Stoughton, 2022
All rights reserved

Series editor: Julia Bird
Produced by Tall Tree Ltd
Editor: Lara Murphy
Designer: Ed Simkins
Writer: Jon Richards
Artist: Josy Bloggs

HB ISBN: 978 1 4451 7048 0
PB ISBN: 978 1 4451 7049 7

Franklin Watts
An imprint of Hachette Children's Group
Part of Hodder and Stoughton
Carmelite House
50 Victoria Embankment
London EC4Y 0DZ

An Hachette UK Company
www.hachette.co.uk
www.hachettechildrens.co.uk

Printed in China

The websites (URLs) included in this book were valid at the time of going to press. However, it is possible that the contents or addresses may have changed since the publication of this book. No responsibility for any such changes can be accepted by either the author or the Publisher.

MIX
Paper | Supporting responsible forestry
FSC® C104740

Contents

4-5
A world of habitats

6-7
Tropical rainforest

8-9
Temperate rainforest

10-11
Desert

12-13
Mountains

14-15
Scrubland

16-17
Rivers and lakes

18-19
Temperate grassland

20-21
Tropical grassland

22-23
Temperate forest

24-25
Forests of Eurasia

26-27
The tundra

28-29
The Arctic

30-32
Glossary
And index

A world of habitats

Earth is a planet of huge contrasts, from arid desert to dense forest and icy polar regions. These variations produce a broad range of habitats, each with their own amazing plants and animals.

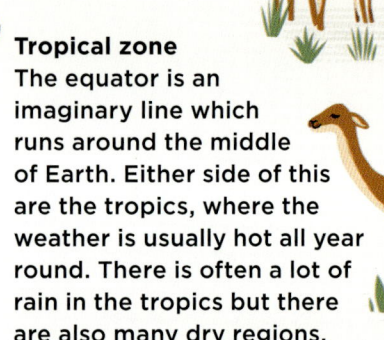

Tropical zone
The equator is an imaginary line which runs around the middle of Earth. Either side of this are the tropics, where the weather is usually hot all year round. There is often a lot of rain in the tropics but there are also many dry regions.

Temperate zone
The temperate zones are found to the north and south of the tropics. Regions in this zone usually experience four seasons in a year – spring, summer, autumn and winter.

 **56.7°C**
– the highest temperature ever recorded on Earth at Furnace Creek, California, USA

 **-89.2°C**
– the lowest temperature ever recorded on Earth at Vostok Station, Antarctica

 Cherrapunji, India, is the place with the most rainfall in a year. During 1860–1861, **26,470 MM** of rain fell.

Polar zone

The polar zones lie at the northern and southern limits of the world. Conditions here can be very cold, especially during winter when the Sun may not rise for days at a time.

Extreme habitats

Living things have evolved to survive in some of the most extreme conditions on the planet. These include the scorching heat of deserts, crushing pressures at the bottom of the ocean or the freezing cold of polar regions.

Environmental changes

Changes in climate lead to changes in habitats. Some regions now have irregular rainfall, with long periods of drought or torrential rains that cause flooding. Other cold regions are getting warmer, which leads to glaciers melting.

Polar zone
Temperate zone
Tropical zone
Temperate zone
Polar zone

29% THE AMOUNT OF EARTH'S SURFACE THAT IS COVERED BY LAND

Of this, **31 per cent** is covered by desert (including the North and South Poles)...

... **33 per cent** is covered by grassland

... and **36 per cent** is covered by forest.

Tropical rainforest
THE AMAZON

Tropical rainforests are found in parts of the world that are warm and very wet. The biggest rainforest in the world is found in the Amazon River basin in South America.

Layered life
At the top of the rainforest are the tallest trees, which poke above the next layer, the canopy. Below the canopy is the understorey, made up of shrubs and small trees. At the bottom is the dark forest floor.

Forest plants
Many rainforest plants don't grow on the ground. These are known as epiphytes and they live on other plants. Rainforest trees include Brazil-nut trees and palms.

Flooding river
Every year, the Amazon River floods almost 250,000 square km of the forest. Tiny zooplankton are carried onto the flooded forest floor and attract fish and other predators.

Forest animals

There are millions of species of rainforest bugs and invertebrates, from tiny leaf-cutter ants to giant bird-eating spiders. Living in the branches are amphibians, such as poison dart frogs, and reptiles, such as boas. Mammals include giant otters and jaguars, while colourful macaws soar above the trees.

Dwindling forest

In the last 40 years, more than 18 per cent of the forest has been cleared to make room for homes and industry. Climate change has led to drier conditions, causing forest fires. This habitat loss threatens the survival of many species.

6.7 MILLION SQUARE KM

THE AREA OF THE AMAZON RAINFOREST

The Amazon accounts for about

HALF

of the world's tropical forest.

THE RAINFOREST IS HOME TO ONE IN TEN SPECIES ON EARTH. THESE INCLUDE:

80,000 plant species (of which 16,000 are trees)

2.5 million insect species

3,000 species of freshwater fish

Nearly 1,300 bird species

370 species of reptile

More than **400** mammal species

Temperate rainforest
LAND OF THE GIANTS

Temperate rainforests are found in cooler regions, where there is lots of rain. The Pacific coast of North America is home to one of the largest temperate rainforests on the planet.

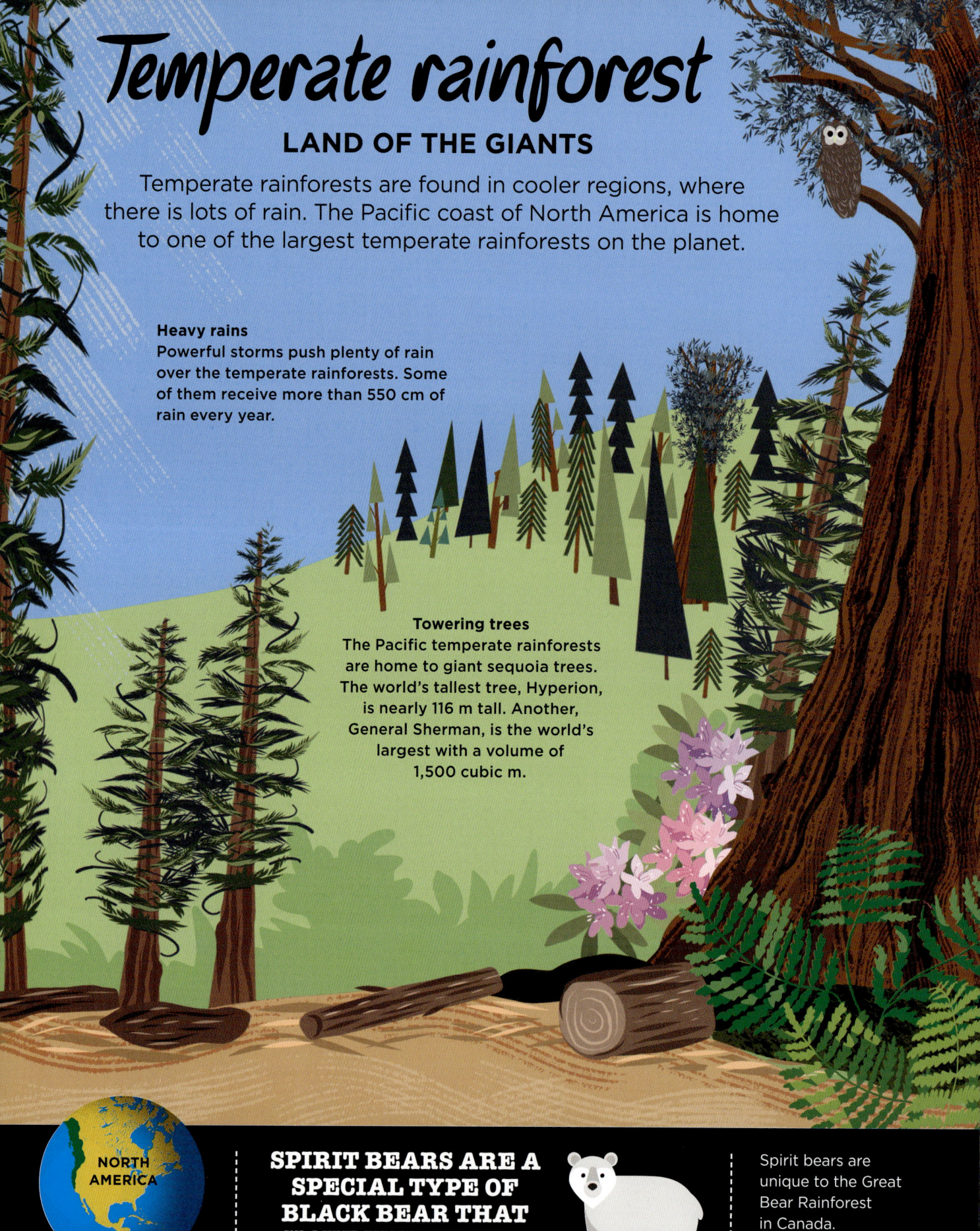

Heavy rains
Powerful storms push plenty of rain over the temperate rainforests. Some of them receive more than 550 cm of rain every year.

Towering trees
The Pacific temperate rainforests are home to giant sequoia trees. The world's tallest tree, Hyperion, is nearly 116 m tall. Another, General Sherman, is the world's largest with a volume of 1,500 cubic m.

NORTH AMERICA

SPIRIT BEARS ARE A SPECIAL TYPE OF BLACK BEAR THAT HAVE WHITE FUR.

Spirit bears are unique to the Great Bear Rainforest in Canada.

Rainforest birds
Located close to coasts, these rainforests are home to seabirds, such as brown pelicans. Further inland are freshwater birds, such as ospreys and great blue herons. Birds of prey include the northern spotted owl and the bald eagle.

The forest floor
Ferns thrive on the damp forest floor and mosses and fungi cover fallen tree trunks, which are home to hundreds of species of invertebrate.

Rainforest mammals
Mammals include northern flying squirrels, mountain beavers, deer and elk, as well as predators, such as coyote and cougars. Temperate rainforests are also home to black bears.

MOUNTAIN LIONS, BEARS AND WOLVES ARE AMONG THE BIGGEST TEMPERATE RAINFOREST PREDATORS.

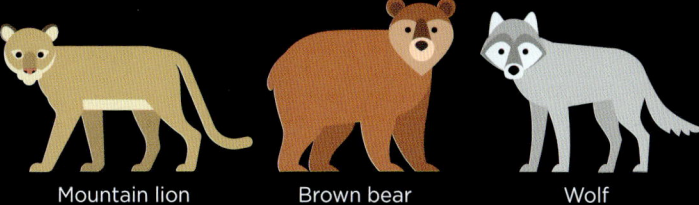

Mountain lion   Brown bear   Wolf

A MOUNTAIN LION CAN GROW TO BE OVER **1.8 M LONG.**

Desert
ARID ATACAMA

Situated on the western edge of South America is the driest place on the planet. The Atacama Desert sits in the shadow of the towering Andes and stretches for about 1,000 km from north to south.

Rain shadow
The Atacama Desert is found between two chains of mountains – the Andes to the east and the Cordillera de la Costa to the west. Any wet air is forced up the mountains and the water it carries is dumped as rain on the mountainsides, leaving only dry air to reach the Atacama.

Dry and barren
Much of the desert floor is covered by stones, sand and salt pans – large areas of salt left behind after any water has evaporated.

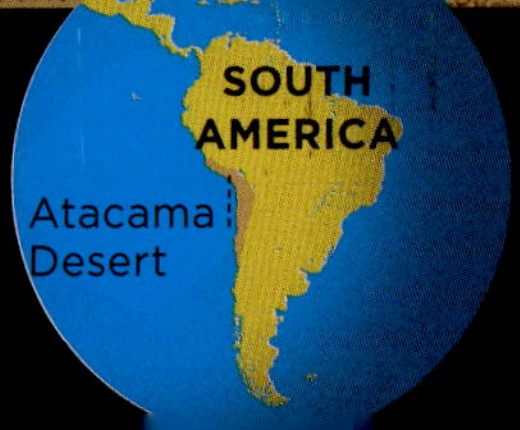

On average, the Atacama receives just 15 mm of rain a year.

SOME WEATHER STATIONS IN THE ATACAMA HAVE RECORDED NO RAINFALL AT ALL.

Clear sky
The dry, cloudless air, and the high altitude of the Atacama make it the perfect place to study the night sky. With little light pollution, the view of the stars at night is pin-sharp.

Coping with the dry
Few animals can survive such extreme conditions. Migrating birds visit seasonally to feed. Invertebrates include desert wasps and red scorpions. Andean flamingos eat algae in the salt flats, while Humboldt penguins live on the coast. Mammals include the Darwin's leaf-eared mouse and the South American grey fox. In grassy areas, there are small herds of guanacos and vicuñas.

Rainfall bloom
Few plants live in the desert climate. These include herbs and flowers, such as thyme and saltgrass. Spiky cacti can live here, and even some trees, such as the pimiento. When rain does fall, the desert becomes carpeted with flowers that emerge to make the most of the water.

THE ATACAMA IS THE OLDEST DESERT ON EARTH, HAVING EXPERIENCED DRY CONDITIONS FOR ABOUT **150 MILLION YEARS**

TEMPERATURES DURING THE DAY IN THE ATACAMA DESERT CAN REACH 40°C, BUT DROP TO JUST 5°C AT NIGHT.

SOME PARTS OF THE DESERT ARE SO DRY THAT NO ANIMALS OR PLANTS CAN SURVIVE THERE

Mountains
TOWERING KILIMANJARO

Towering over the African grasslands, Kilimanjaro is a dormant volcano and the tallest mountain in Africa. Travelling up the sides of the mountain takes you through a number of climate bands, each with its own distinct plant and animal life.

Disappearing snow
Climate change is having an effect on Kilimanjaro. Since 1912, the snow caps at the mountain's peak have lost more than 80 per cent of their mass as the snow melts away.

Alpine desert zone
The zone between 4,000 and 5,000 m receives less than 250 mm of rain a year, making it a desert.

Arctic zone
Scree slopes, made up of loose stones, form the start of this zone, before giving way to the snow-covered peak.

Scrubland

THE AUSTRALIAN OUTBACK

Stretching across much of the interior of Australia is a vast region called the Outback. This is a mixture of desert and arid scrubland where a diverse range of plants and animals live.

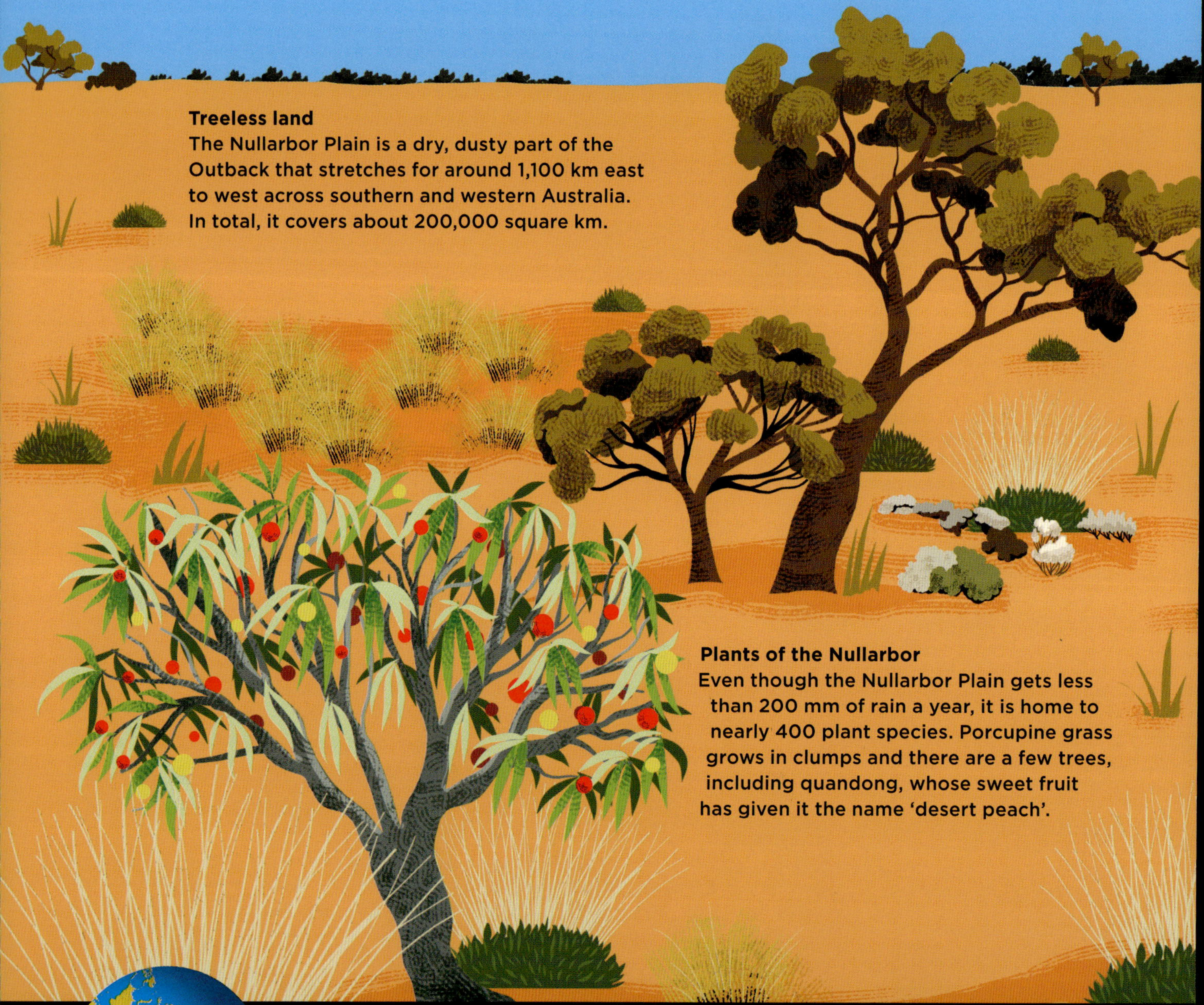

Treeless land
The Nullarbor Plain is a dry, dusty part of the Outback that stretches for around 1,100 km east to west across southern and western Australia. In total, it covers about 200,000 square km.

Plants of the Nullarbor
Even though the Nullarbor Plain gets less than 200 mm of rain a year, it is home to nearly 400 plant species. Porcupine grass grows in clumps and there are a few trees, including quandong, whose sweet fruit has given it the name 'desert peach'.

AUSTRALIA

THE OUTBACK COVERS
6.5 MILLION SQUARE KM
OF THE CENTRE OF AUSTRALIA. THIS VAST AREA IS HOME TO JUST 10 PER CENT OF AUSTRALIA'S POPULATION.

The word 'Nullarbor' comes from the Latin words meaning 'no tree'.

Outback mammals

Several species of large mammals can be found wandering the Nullarbor. These include herds of feral (wild) camels and wild dogs called dingos which scavenge to survive. Red kangaroos live in groups called mobs and feed off any fresh vegetation they can find.

Small animals

Bird life in the Nullarbor Plain is diverse and includes scavengers, such as the Australian raven and seed-eaters, such as the Mulga parrot. On the ground, southern hard-nosed wombats dig burrows to escape the heat, while the Nullarbor bearded dragon is well camouflaged in the scrub.

 AROUND 1 MILLION FERAL CAMELS LIVE IN AUSTRALIA, MAKING IT HOME TO THE WORLD'S LARGEST POPULATION OF WILD CAMELS.

RED KANGAROOS CAN BOUND ALONG AT ABOUT 55 KPH AND JUMP NEARLY 2 M VERTICALLY.

Rivers and lakes

THE MISSISSIPPI

The Mississippi River and its tributaries, including the Missouri River, form one of the world's largest river systems. It drains a huge part of the North American continent, running through a wide range of habitats.

Source
The source of the Mississippi is Lake Itasca in Minnesota. From here, the river winds through a range of forests, grasslands and wetlands, as well as cities, including St Louis and New Orleans.

River plants
Plants change as the river winds along its course. Tall prairie grasses and flowers give way to forests of maple and oak.

Fish
The river is home to hundreds of fish species, including carp, smallmouth bass, American eels and paddlefish.

NORTH AMERICA
Gulf of Mexico

THE MISSOURI-MISSISSIPPI RIVER NETWORK IS **5,970 KM LONG** MAKING IT THE FOURTH LONGEST RIVER NETWORK IN THE WORLD.

The Mississippi drains water from 32 US states and 2 Canadian provinces, and has a river basin covering 3.2 million square km – the fourth largest in the world.

Temperate grassland
THE GREAT PLAINS

From the feet of the Rocky Mountains, the lush Great Plains stretch east for about 1,000 km, and run for more than 4,500 km from central Canada and through the USA down almost to the border with Mexico.

Great grasses
This habitat was once a sea of tall grasses. Much of these have been destroyed by farming. Dotted here and there among the grasses that remain are shrubs and small trees, such as cottonwood.

Disappearing grazers
The Great Plains used to be grazed by huge herds of bison and pronghorn. Hunting and habitat loss have reduced their numbers considerably.

NORTH AMERICA
The Great Plains

2.9 MILLION SQUARE KM
– THE APPROXIMATE AREA OF THE GREAT PLAINS.

570 MILLION YEARS AGO, THE GREAT PLAINS WERE AN INTERNAL SEA, WHICH IS WHY THE LAND IS SO FLAT TODAY.

Tropical grassland
THE SERENGETI

This large African grassland region is home to some of the world's most amazing animals. The Serengeti is under threat, but protected areas and national parks should help to preserve it.

Grasses and trees
The Serengeti has two types of region – woodland and grassland. The treeless grassland areas are dominated by long grasses, while the woodlands are dotted with trees, such as acacia.

Great grazers
The Serengeti is the perfect home for grazing animals. Wildebeest eat short grasses, while zebras feed on longer ones. Small antelopes called dik-diks eat the lowest leaves, while impalas feed on the higher ones, leaving giraffes to stretch up to eat the topmost leaves.

Growing cities
While grasslands in the protected parts remain intact, other grasslands have been swallowed up by growing towns and cities.

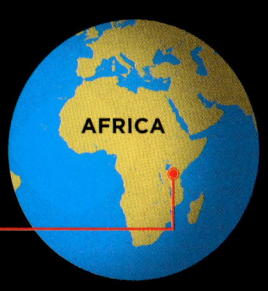

AFRICA

Lake Victoria
Serengeti National Park

18,000 SQUARE KM
APPROXIMATE AREA OF THE SERENGETI

Bird life
Birds of the Serengeti include long-legged ostriches that can run at up to 70 kph and secretary birds that kill snakes by stamping on them with their razor-sharp claws.

THE SERENGETI IS HOME TO:

1.3 MILLION wildebeest

200,000 plains zebra

400,000 Thomson's gazelle

THERE ARE OVER
200
TYPES OF GRASS IN THE SERENGETI.

CHEETAHS CAN RUN AT SPEEDS OF UP TO
120 KPH.

On the prowl
The herds of grazing animals attract predators, including lions, spotted hyenas and cheetahs. Human hunters pose an additional threat to grazing animals, as well as their predators.

Temperate forest
FORESTS OF NORTHERN EUROPE

Białowieża Forest is a densely wooded region that straddles the Poland–Belarus border. This habitat is different to temperate rainforests because of the lower rainfall.

Dense forest
Many of the trees that make up the forest are hundreds of years old. As well as conifers and other evergreen trees, there are elms, limes and ancient oaks.

Forest paradise
Much of the forest is left undisturbed, which means that there are plenty of dead trees littering the forest floor. These make a perfect home for fungi and bugs that are attracted to the damp, decaying wood.

1,500 SQUARE KM
APPROXIMATE AREA OF BIAŁOWIEŻA FOREST

THE FOREST IS HOME TO **59 MAMMAL SPECIES, 250 TYPES OF BIRD, 13 SPECIES OF AMPHIBIAN, 7 SPECIES OF REPTILE** AND MORE THAN **12,000 SPECIES OF INVERTEBRATE.**

Life in the trees
Mammals range from wood mice to wild boar and red deer, and are hunted by predators such as lynxes and wolves. In the trees, woodpeckers and flycatchers feed on insects, while owls and eagles hunt small mammals.

Big bison
Europe's largest land mammal, the European bison, was once hunted to extinction in the forest. Bison have been gradually reintroduced to the forest from zoos, and today the herd numbers around 900.

Protection
For hundreds of years, the forest has been shrinking due to farming and logging. To protect this precious habitat, the area was made a national park in 1932 and is now a UNESCO World Heritage site.

25 PER CENT OF THE WORLD'S TOTAL POPULATION OF EUROPEAN BISON LIVE HERE.

Almost 50 per cent of the wood in the forest is dead, providing homes for thousands of species.

Forests of Eurasia
THE TAIGA

Stretching across the top of Asia, Europe and North America is an enormous band of forest called taiga. Also known as boreal forest, it is made up of coniferous trees, such as pines, spruces and larches.

Trees of the taiga
Most of the trees in the taiga are evergreen. These trees keep their leaves all year round so they can make the most of the sunlight, even during short winter days.

Forest floor
The forest floor is shaded by the trees above, keeping it dark all year round. It is also covered by the dead needles that the trees shed. Lichens and fungi grow here, and little else.

Temperatures in the taiga can dip below **-50°C** in the winter months.

BOREAL FOREST COVERS ABOUT **11 PER CENT** OF EARTH'S LAND SURFACE.

Human threats
Logging and forest clearing have reduced the size of the taiga over the years, and many parts of this habitat have been cleared for oil drilling. Some animals, such as foxes and wolves, have been hunted for their fur.

Forest birds
While a few birds stay in the forest all year, their numbers soar during the summer when migrating birds, such as Canada geese and warblers, arrive to feed on plants and insects.

Forest animals
Animals living in the taiga have adapted to the cold. Mammals, like bears, lynxes and wolves, have thick coats to keep them warm, and many hibernate through the bitter winter.

FOREST FIRES DESTROY LARGE AREAS OF TAIGA, BUT THEY ALSO CLEAR PARTS OF THE FOREST, ALLOWING NEW TREES TO GROW.

RISING TEMPERATURES DUE TO CLIMATE CHANGE ARE MAKING FOREST FIRES MORE FREQUENT.

The tundra
ICY CANADA

To the north of the boreal forest is a freezing treeless region called the tundra. In winter, the land is an icy wasteland, but during the short summer, the surface melts, flowers bloom and birds arrive to raise young.

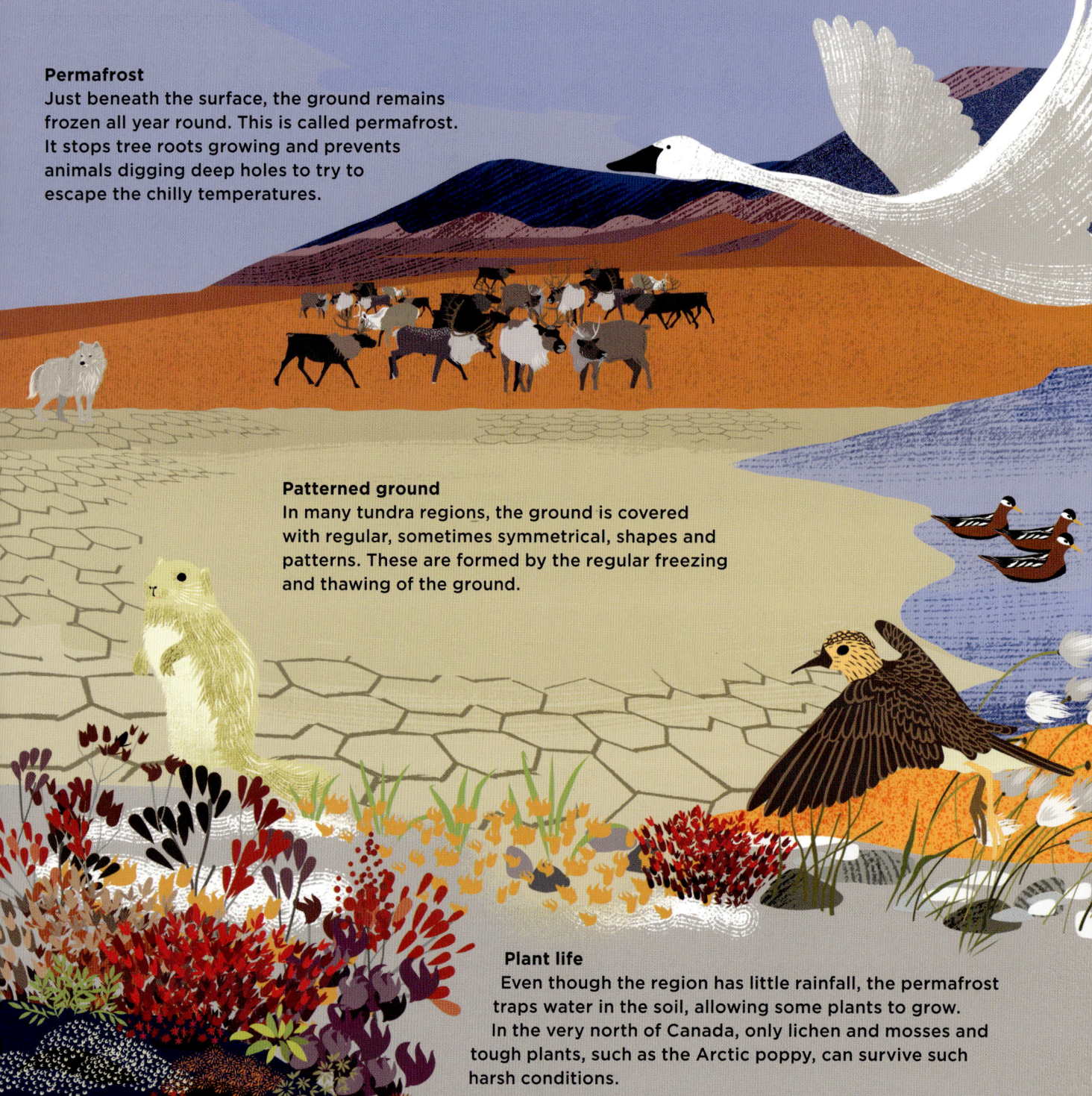

Permafrost
Just beneath the surface, the ground remains frozen all year round. This is called permafrost. It stops tree roots growing and prevents animals digging deep holes to try to escape the chilly temperatures.

Patterned ground
In many tundra regions, the ground is covered with regular, sometimes symmetrical, shapes and patterns. These are formed by the regular freezing and thawing of the ground.

Plant life
Even though the region has little rainfall, the permafrost traps water in the soil, allowing some plants to grow. In the very north of Canada, only lichen and mosses and tough plants, such as the Arctic poppy, can survive such harsh conditions.

Summer visitors

Few birds stay in the tundra all year round. During the brief summer months, however, plenty of birds migrate to the region to breed as plants bloom and insects appear. Visiting birds include ducks, geese and terns.

Tundra animals

Most mammals on the tundra are migrators, such as caribou. Mammals that live here all year round include small Arctic ground squirrels and the Arctic wolf.

Changing habitats

Due to global warming, animals like the red fox are moving north into the tundra and competing with native species. Shrubs are thriving, crowding out lichens – a favourite food of the tundra's herds of caribou.

CLOSE TO THE ARCTIC CIRCLE, PERMAFROST CAN STRETCH MORE THAN **600 M** UNDER THE GROUND.

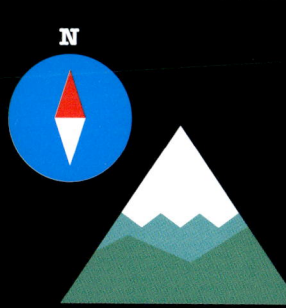

THERE ARE TWO TYPES OF TUNDRA – ARCTIC TUNDRA, WHICH LIES CLOSE TO THE NORTH POLE, AND ALPINE TUNDRA, WHICH IS FOUND HIGH IN MOUNTAINOUS REGIONS.

The tundra gets very little precipitation (rain or snow) – just 150–250 mm per year. That's less than most of the world's deserts!

A CARIBOU'S HOOVES ARE HARD IN WINTER BUT BECOME SOFTER AND SPONGIER IN SUMMER.

The Arctic
NORTHERN WASTELAND

The Arctic region is dominated by a large ocean that is covered in thick sea ice for much of the year. Surrounding this are the tops of North America, Europe and Asia, as well as hundreds of smaller islands.

Midnight Sun
Earth is tilted as it orbits the Sun. This means that in the depths of winter, the Sun does not rise at all and the Arctic experiences darkness for entire days. During summer, the Sun stays above the horizon, giving the region daylight for several days at a time.

Plant life
Arctic plant life has to cope with freezing temperatures, poor soil and permanently frozen ground. Small shrubs, mosses and algae grow here.

Bird life
The Arctic is home to water birds, such as fulmars, guillemots and eiders. There are a few land-living birds, such as the ptarmigan, as well as birds of prey, including snowy owls.

THE ARCTIC

THE ARCTIC IS HOME TO:

280 TYPES OF BIRD

450 FISH SPECIES

130 MAMMAL SPECIES

Mammals

Coastal areas are home to seals, sea lions and walruses. These attract predators, including polar bears and orcas. Reindeer and huge musk ox live inland, as well as Arctic foxes and hares.

Disappearing ice

As climate change pushes global temperatures up, more of the sea ice is melting. With less pack ice to hunt on, polar bears are forced to travel to find food wherever they can, including in towns and villages.

The name 'Arctic' comes from the Greek word 'arktos' meaning 'bear' and refers to the northern constellation Ursa Major, the Great Bear.

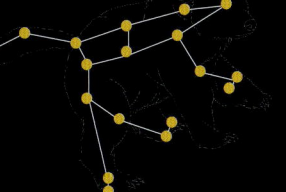

ARCTIC FOXES AND HARES CHANGE THE COLOUR OF THEIR COATS, FROM WHITE IN WINTER TO BROWN IN SUMMER.

Glossary

Algae a type of plant that grows in water or damp conditions and has no stem or leaves

Arid describes land that receives little or no rain

Biodiversity the variety of plant and animal species in a habitat

Boreal forest a type of forest that is made up of coniferous trees, such as spruces and pines

Broadleaf tree a tree that has wide leaves rather than needles

Canopy the layer of branches and leaves formed by trees in a forest

Climate change the changes in Earth's climate that scientists believe are caused by increases in greenhouse gases, such as carbon dioxide and methane

Coniferous mostly evergreen trees that produce cones which carry seeds

Delta the area where a river meets another body of water, for example the sea

Desert an area that receives less than 250 mm of precipitation a year

Drought a long period with very little rain

Epiphyte a type of plant that grows on another plant instead of on the ground

Equator an imaginary line that runs around the widest part of Earth, midway between the two poles

Evergreen a type of tree that does not lose its leaves in winter

Extinction when a species of living thing dies out

Fungi types of living things that include tiny organisms such as mould and mushrooms

Hibernate when an animal enters a sleep-like state to slow down its body processes and preserve energy during the winter months

Insulate to protect something from the cold. Animals insulate themselves with thick layers of fat beneath the skin and thick furry coats

Invertebrate a type of animal, such as an insect or a spider, that does not have a spine

Lichen a simple, low-lying plant that often grows on rocks and tree bark

Mammal a warm-blooded animal that has a backbone and grows hair at some stage of its life

---

FURTHER INFORMATION

WEBSITES
www.natgeokids.com
www.nasa.gov/kidsclub
www.oceanservice.noaa.gov/kids/

MUSEUMS

Science Museum
Exhibition Road, South Kensington, London SW7 2DD

Oxford University Museum of Natural History
Parks Rd, Oxford, OX1 3PW

Migrate an animal's movement from one place to another for feeding or breeding

Permafrost a layer found just below the surface of the tundra that is permanently frozen all year round

Poles the regions that lie at the top and bottom of Earth. The region around the North Pole is called the Arctic, while the region around the South Pole is called Antarctica

Predator an animal that hunts, kills and eats other animals

Prey animals that are killed and eaten by predators

Rainforest a type of forest that receives a lot of rain

Scavenge searching for discarded and decaying materials to feed on

Scree part of a mountain slope that is covered by loose stones

Sediment tiny particles of stone or grains of sand that are carried by water, for example by a river

Species a group of living things that share characteristics and can reproduce

Taiga the large belt of forest that stretches across the top of North America, Europe and Asia

Temperate the regions of the world that lie between the tropics and the polar regions

Thawing another name for melting

Tree line the point on a mountain or close to the poles beyond which trees will not grow

Tributaries smaller streams and rivers that flow into larger ones

Tropical the regions of the world that lie on either side of the equator

Tundra areas found high up mountains or close to the poles where no trees grow and the ground is frozen all year

Zooplankton tiny creatures that live in water

BOOKS
World Feature Focus series by Rebecca Kahn (Franklin Watts, 2020).
Discover some of the most famous and important habitats on the planet with key facts, illustrations and photos.

Expedition Diaries series by Simon Chapman (Franklin Watts, 2018).
Explore fascinating habitats around the world with information, sketches and photos inspired by real-life travel.

Index

algae 28
Amazon rainforest 6-7
Arctic 28-29
Atacama Desert 10-11

bearded dragons 15
bears 8, 9, 17, 25, 29
Białowieża Forest 22-23
biodiversity 6
birdlife 7, 9, 11, 15, 17, 21, 23, 25, 27, 28
birds of prey 9, 17, 23, 28
bison 18, 19, 23
boreal forest 24

cacti 11
camels 15
caribou 27
cheetahs 21
climate change 5, 7, 12, 19, 25, 27, 29
coniferous trees 22, 24

deltas 17
deserts 5, 10-11, 12, 14
droughts 5, 19

epiphytes 6
equator 4
evergreen trees 22, 24
extinction 19, 23
extreme habitats 5

farming 18, 19, 23
ferns 9

fish 7, 16, 17, 28
flooding 5, 6, 19
forest fires 7, 25
forests 5, 6-9, 13, 16, 22-25
foxes 11, 27, 29
fungi 9, 22, 24

giant sequoia trees 8
grasslands 5, 13, 16, 18-21
Great Plains 18-19

habitat loss 7, 18, 19, 23, 25
hibernation 25
hunting 18, 19, 21, 23, 25

ice, melting 5, 29

kangaroos 15
Kilimanjaro 12-13

lichens 24, 26, 27

migrations 11, 17, 25, 27
Mississippi River 16-17
Missouri-Mississippi river network 16
mosses 9, 26, 28
mountain lions 9
mountains 10, 12-13

Nullarbor Plain 14-15

Outback 14-15

permafrost 26

polar zones 5, 28-29
prairie dogs 19

rainfall 4, 5, 8, 10, 11, 12, 14, 22, 27
rainforests 6-9
rivers and lakes 16-17

salt pans 10
scavengers 15
scrubland 14-15
seasons 4
Serengeti 20-21

taiga 24-25
temperate forests 22-23
temperate grasslands 18-19
temperate rainforests 8-9
temperate zones 4
temperatures 4, 11, 13, 24
tropical grasslands 20-21
tropical rainforests 6-7
tropics 4
tundra 26-27

volcanic activity 13

wildebeest 21
wildlife 7, 8-9, 11, 13, 15, 16, 17, 18, 19, 20, 21, 22-23, 25, 27, 28-29
wolves 9, 23, 25, 27
wombats 15

zebras 13, 20, 21